SONG IN A RAINSTORM

The STORY of MUSICAL PRODIGY
THOMAS *"Blind Tom"* WIGGINS

GLENDA ARMAND   *illustrated by* BRITTANY JACKSON

ALBERT WHITMAN & COMPANY
Chicago, Illinois

His mother, Charity, slowly shook her head as she cradled him in her arms. Mingo, his father, paced the dirt floor in silence. They knew what would be expected of their son when he grew up. The same that would be expected of any black baby born in 1849 on a Georgia plantation: Chop wood in the freezing cold. Pick cotton in the scorching heat. Obey or be punished with the whip, the auction block—or worse.

What would Master Jones do when he discovered Baby Tom was blind?

Mingo and Charity Wiggins did not have long to wait for an answer. Jones sold the whole family to a nearby farmer, General James Bethune. Jones included the baby free of charge.

After Charity and Mingo found out that Wiley Jones planned to sell some of his slaves, they sought out General James Bethune, whom they considered to be a "fair man." Their goal was twofold: to keep their family together and their blind son alive.

When Wiley Jones sold the Wiggins family to Bethune, Jones had no idea that Charity and Mingo had prearranged the sale.

Charity held Baby Tom close as she and her family bumped along in General Bethune's wagon to their new home. She knew her baby was not a "useless burden," as Master Jones had called him. But even Charity could not imagine that one day her son would be called a musical wonder.

From birth, Baby Tom's sense of hearing was remarkable. He giggled and cooed at the things he heard: his mother's singing, a crackling fire, pots and pans rattling.

As he grew, Baby Tom delighted in creating his own noise. He pinched his sisters to hear them squeal. He climbed atop the table and shoved off dishes.

Clank, clatter, crash!

Baby Tom clapped with glee.

Mingo built a wooden crate and put it in the
middle of their cabin. Inside, his headstrong son
could sleep, play, and stay out of trouble.

But sounds swirled around Baby Tom, beckoning him to follow.

And he did. Out of the crate and out the door. Day or night, rain or shine.

One morning the *drip, drip, drip* of a steady downpour drew

Baby Tom onto the porch. The rain's melody lured him too close to the edge.

He fell headfirst into a bucket of water! His mother rescued him just in time.

While Tom was undeterred, his family was worried. His siblings wondered why their little brother did not talk or "behave." Charity explained that Tom was not misbehaving. He was different from other children. Charity gave Tom's sisters the task of fetching their brother when he wandered off.

With his sisters in pursuit, Little Tom continued his search for new sounds. He toddled to the fence surrounding the cabin. He climbed up, listened, then echoed what he heard.

He **whinnied** with the horse,

crowed with the rooster,

and **hooted** with the owl, all with perfect pitch.

Soon, the fence proved no match for Tom's curiosity. Distant voices led him to an open window of the Big House. Inside, General Bethune's daughters had gathered to sing and play instruments.

On this day, the sisters received a big surprise when they stopped singing: their song continued without them!

Four-year-old Tom became the eager student of a quartet of teachers. After just a few lessons, he could belt out every song the sisters knew. But, as always, Tom was simply mimicking sounds.

One evening, after the children had sung for the family, General Bethune declared that if Tom could sing, he could speak. The general walked over to the little boy.

Tom heard, "Sit down, Tom." At the same time, he felt himself being guided onto a chair. Then, as he was being lifted from the chair, Tom heard, "Stand up."

Tom smiled. He understood.

The sisters jumped into action. One by one, they handed Tom an object while pronouncing its name. Excitedly, Tom felt and smelled each object, repeated its name, and never forgot it.

Little Tom continued to discover and learn. He was fascinated by the instrument Mary, the oldest sister, played. Touching, sniffing, listening, Tom explored every inch of the huge object. He sat on the bench and found the keys. He banged on them with his hands and elbows.

The girls covered their ears. What a cacophony!

Tom kept playing, using only his fingers. As he struck
the keys, he realized that each had its own voice.
The cacophony transformed into a familiar melody.

Seeing a business opportunity, General Bethune
decided that Tom would live in the Big House. Tearfully,
Charity walked Tom to his new home. Her son was still
enslaved, but at least for now, he would be safe. Still, she
would miss him. And in her heart, Charity knew that
Tom would never again live with his family.

That day, Tom began his new life with his very own piano. Mary grounded him in the basics. He took lessons from tutors. Then he soared on his own.

Seated at the piano, Tom entered into his own world. In it, he spent up to twelve hours a day. When he was there, Tom was not "different." He belonged.

When Tom did stray from the piano, he frolicked outdoors.

He moved with ease through scented flowers and trees.

Oh, the joy of spinning, eyes closed and chin up! Feeling the sun's warm embrace or the rain's soft kisses on his face.

Nature spoke to him, and he responded on the piano.

"What are you playing, Tom?" someone would ask.

"What the trees said to me," his answer might be, or,

"It's what the birdies sang to me."

During one fierce storm, Tom made his way back
and forth between the piano and a tin-roofed passageway.

Rain danced on the roof. Tom's fingers danced on the keys:
Plink, plink, plink!

Lightning cracked, and Tom thundered:
Boom! Boom! Boom!

A short time later, family, friends, and workers peered through windows and doors, and gathered in the parlor to listen to the six-year-old play his first composition: *Rainstorm*.

To Tom's delight, everyone cheered and hooted and clapped.

General Bethune announced that Tom would become a professional musician.

Billed as "Blind Tom," he performed in his home state of Georgia and throughout the South. Some people went to see Tom's show doubting his ability: *There must be trickery involved. After all, how could a blind, enslaved boy master the piano?*

But, although Tom was unpredictable and might
not stick to the program, his talent always shone through.
He played requests and songs he had composed. He made his
piano *rat-a-tat-tat* like a drum, *chirp* like a sparrow,
and *twang* like a banjo.

By the end of the show, doubters had become believers.

News of the child prodigy reached Washington, DC. In 1860,
when Tom was eleven years old, he played for President James Buchanan.
Tom was the first African American artist to perform at the White House.

Even as the Civil War raged, Southerners lined up at concert halls to pay fifty cents to attend Tom's performances.

The Audience Challenge was a crowd favorite. Someone would come on stage and play a piece of music. Whether it was long or short, classical or created on the spot, Tom listened intently and then repeated the piece note for note.

For his finale, Tom played one song with his left hand and another with his right, all while singing a third in perfect harmony!

In 1863, when James Bethune saw the end of the Civil War and of slavery on the horizon, he entered into a contract with Tom's parents. They would receive $500 a year from Tom's income, a good sum at a time when the average white farm laborer earned less than $200 per year. However, Bethune paid himself one hundred times the amount he gave Tom's parents.

In 1865 the war ended, and slavery was abolished. Although he was no longer enslaved, Tom's life continued much as before. For him, freedom meant creating music from the world around him. With freedom, his world became bigger.

Along with his tutor, assistant, and General Bethune, Tom traveled by rail across the United States and Canada. His love of trains led Tom to create a special act for his show. He combined his voice, "*chuh-chuh-chuh*," with piano chords, *clang-clang-clang-clang*. His impression was so realistic that in your mind's eye you saw a train coming!

Besides his great musical gifts, Tom possessed odd habits such as spinning, hopping, and mimicking speakers. He was in constant motion. Even when he got older and heavier, Tom liked to hop about on one leg with the other parallel to the floor, maintaining perfect balance.

Some people mocked and dismissed Tom because of his unusual behavior. But when Tom sat down to play, his genius was clear.

Everywhere he performed, Young Tom played classical pieces and popular ditties. He added new routines and kept crowd-pleasers. Once, in Alabama, an accomplished pianist played a piece for The Audience Challenge. Tom smiled and listened.

When the pianist finished, Tom said, "I'll play the number as the lady played it." After doing so, Tom announced, "Now I will play the number as the lady should have played it."

And he did, hitting all the notes that the pianist had missed.

Mingo and Charity were proud of their son. But, sadly, because of his travels, they rarely saw him. Their consolation was that Tom had proven what they had known all along. He was not a burden but a gift.

In her later years, Charity was able to spend a few months on tour with Tom. Those days, she recalled, were "as near heaven" as she would ever get "this side of the real heaven."

Before long, Tom was an international celebrity.
At seventeen, he set sail for Europe.

General Bethune explained to Tom that commoners and
royalty would come to see him with one question on their
minds: *Was this blind former slave truly the greatest living musician?*

Tom was eager to answer with his piano. He gave a flawless performance of a difficult piece, Beethoven's Third Piano Concerto. The crowd shouted its approval, "Bravo! Bravo!"

But Tom was not done. He had impressed them. Now he would transport them.

Tom played the *Concerto* again, this time with his back to the piano. Left hand playing the right hand part and vice versa. He did not miss a beat. At the final note, people sat in stunned silence. *Impossible.* Yet they had witnessed it with their own eyes and ears.

Tom stood facing the audience. Finally, he heard the theater erupt into thunderous applause. Cheers rang out. Tom trembled at the sound. Tears streaming, he took a bow. This was his world. And he reigned.

Tom's European tour was the highlight of a career that spanned half a century. Many thousands of people around the world attended his performances. How fortunate they were to experience the genius of Thomas Wiggins:

To board Tom's piano train and joyfully ride along,
    as Charity's son, the musical wonder,
    turned a rainstorm into a song.

Author's Note

THOMAS WIGGINS was born blind to enslaved parents near Columbus, Georgia, on May 25, 1849. Had he been born in our time, he might have been called an autistic musical savant.

However, to his original owner, Tom was a defective piece of property. Slave owners had complete authority over their slaves, including the power to decide whether they lived or died.

Tom's wise and loving mother, Charity Wiggins, played an instrumental role in her son's survival and in his unlikely career. Charity sought out James Bethune because he had a reputation as a "fair man."

At the time, Charity did not know that the Bethunes were a musical family or that Tom had a musical gift. And his gift was astounding. It combined an incredible memory and focus with physical agility and creativity. His natural ability was enhanced by piano lessons from the finest teachers of his day. Tom could master in an hour what might take other students weeks to learn. He was also a fine singer and prolific composer and songwriter.

For all his talents, Tom never fully understood the legal battles that were fought over him most of his life. The battles were for guardianship of Tom and rights to the fortune he earned. While Tom was well taken care of, much of his money went to pay a long line of managers, guardians, piano tutors, lawyers, and caregivers. James Bethune's family and other opportunists became wealthy on Tom's talent.

His parents, especially Charity, who gave birth to at least twelve children, never gave up their legal fight over guardianship, visitation, and a larger share of Tom's earnings.

Mingo Wiggins died in 1873; Charity, who lived to be one hundred, died in 1901.

While exploitation, litigation, and slavery are an important part of Tom's story, *Song in a Rainstorm* shines a well-deserved light on Tom himself, who, in spite of incredible odds, was able to realize his passion in life—making music. It is about a boy, born blind and enslaved, who grew up to be one of the greatest musical prodigies our country has produced.

Tom died of a stroke on June 14, 1908, at the age of fifty-eight. But his story contains a message for children today: Sometimes the thing that makes you different is the very thing that makes you free.

Resources

No original recordings of Tom playing exist today. But some musicians, such as pianist John Davis, have recorded their own versions of Tom's pieces. To hear more, check out *John Davis Plays Blind Tom: The Eighth Wonder*.

Selected Sources

The Marvelous Musical Prodigy, Blind Tom. London: Forgotten Books, 2016.

O'Connell, Deirdre. *The Ballad of Blind Tom, Slave Pianist*. New York: Overlook Press, 2009.

Schley, Jack. "Thomas Wiggins Bethune." *Southern Views Magazine*, May 31, 2018.

Southall, Geneva Handy. *Blind Tom, the Black Pianist-Composer (1849–1908): Continually Enslaved*. Lanham, MD: Scarecrow Press, 1999.

Southall, Geneva Handy. *Blind Tom: The Post Civil War Enslavement of a Black Musical Genius*. Minneapolis: Challenge Books, 1979.

Southall, Geneva Handy. *The Continuing Enslavement of Blind Tom, the Black Pianist-Composer (1865–1887)*. Minneapolis: Challenge Books, 1983.

To all uniquely gifted children, and the adults who teach and love them—GA

To Glenda Armand, I would like to express my gratitude for allowing me
to take part in the telling of Tom's story. This was a wonderful, educational experience
for me, in which I learned about who Tom Wiggins was and heard him play the piano
for the first time. Tom was a true savant, and I am so grateful for the
opportunity to get to know him through your work. —BJ

Library of Congress Cataloging-in-Publication data
is on file with the publisher.

Text copyright © 2021 by Glenda Armand
Illustrations copyright © 2021 by Albert Whitman & Company
Illustrations by Brittany Jackson
First published in the United States of America
in 2021 by Albert Whitman & Company

ISBN 978-0-8075-0941-8 (hardcover)
ISBN 978-0-8075-0946-3 (ebook)

Printed in China
10 9 8 7 6 5 4 3 2 1 RRD 24 23 22 21 20

Design by Aphelandra

For more information about Albert Whitman & Company,
visit our website at www.albertwhitman.com.